A New True Book

HEALTH

By Karen Jacobsen

This "true book" was prepared
under the direction of
Illa Podendorf,
formerly with the Laboratory School,
University of Chicago

CHILDRENS PRESS, CHICAGO

PHOTO CREDITS

Tony Freeman, Photographer— Cover, 2, 4, 7, 9, 10, 12, 13 (2 photos), 14 (2 photos) 15, 17, 19, 20, 21, 23, 24, 25, 26, 27, 28, 30, 32, 34, 35, 37, 38, 39, 41, 42, 43, 44, 45
Ray Bruno Photo—33

Library of Congress Cataloging in Publication Data

Jacobsen, Karen.
  Health.
  (A New true book)
  For grades 1-3.
  Summary: An easy-to-read discussion of what your body needs to remain healthy.
  1. Health—Juvenile literature. [1. Health]
I. Title.
RA777.J25   613'.0432   81-6193
ISBN 0-516-01622-9   AACR2

86-1226

TABLE OF CONTENTS

YOUR BODY AND BRAIN

The human body can do so many things.

It can walk and it can run.

It can hop, skip, or jump.

It can stand up or sit down.

It can stop, look, and listen.

The human body is truly wonderful.

It even has a brain.

The brain thinks and it learns.

The brain has ideas.

You have a body and a brain.

They belong to you.

It's your job to take good care of them.

Do you know how?

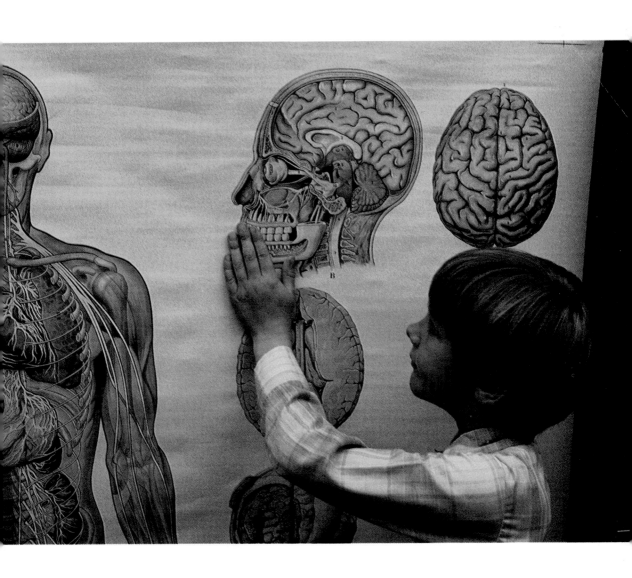

YOUR BODY NEEDS FOOD

Let's start with food.

Your body needs food, at least three or four times a day.

Food helps your body to grow.

Milk and cheese help to
grow teeth and bones.

Meat, fish, and eggs help
to grow muscles and many
other parts of your body.

Food also keeps you going. It helps you to be strong and active.

Your body changes food into energy. You use energy to work and to play.

You need energy for
everything that you do.
Sometimes you only use
a little energy.

But other times you use
a lot of energy.

To keep going, you need
a new supply of food for
energy, every day.

You need food to grow
and food for energy.

But there are so many
kinds of food.

Which foods are the
best for you?

Fruit and vegetables are very important. They taste good and they are good for you. Your body needs at least four servings of fruit or vegetables, every day.

You should eat eggs,
fish, or meat at least twice
a day.

Foods made from milk
are very good for you. You
should drink a glass of
milk with every meal.

Many foods are made from grains, such as wheat, corn, and rice. You should eat four or more servings of grain foods every day.

Every meal that you eat should contain some of these good foods.

Together, they give your body what it needs to go and to grow.

You should start each day with a good breakfast.

First, have some juice or fruit.

Then, try eggs and toast
or cereal with raisins.
Don't forget to drink a
glass of milk.

For lunch, have a
tuna fish salad sandwich
with carrot and celery
sticks or try vegetable
soup with cheese toast.
    Drink your milk and have
an apple for dessert.

For dinner, you can eat chicken, peas, rice, salad, and a roll.

Or try meatloaf with potatoes, string beans, and tomatoes.

Ice cream is always good for dessert.

Good food keeps your body going and growing.

But some kinds of food are not good for you. Try not to eat them very often.

YOUR BODY
NEEDS TO WORK

Eating good food will
build your body.

But it needs exercise to
make it strong and healthy.

Your body needs to
move. It needs to stretch,
bend, lift, push, and pull.

YOUR BODY
NEEDS TO REST

After exercising, you should rest for a while. Sit down. Cool off. Take a short nap if you are really tired.

At night you need a long rest. You should sleep at least ten hours every night. Too little sleep can make you sick.

A good night's sleep helps to keep you healthy.

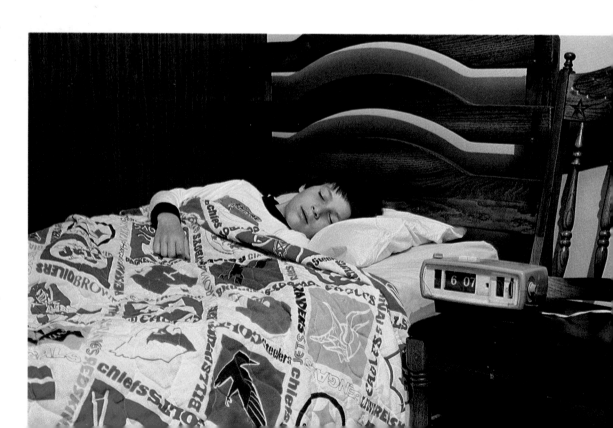

YOUR BODY
NEEDS PROTECTION

During the day you come and go.

Sometimes you are inside.

Other times you are outside.

What clothes should you wear?

On hot days loose
clothing is the most
comfortable. It lets you
move freely.

On cold days you should
wear layers of clothes. The
layers trap your body heat
and keep you warm.

On rainy days you need
protection from the rain.
Special clothes will help to
keep you dry.

TAKE CARE
OF YOUR BODY

Every day you need
clean clothes. Clean
clothes are nice to wear.
They make you feel good
and they help to keep you
healthy.

A clean body is important, too. You should take a bath or a shower, every day. Wash your hair at least once a week.

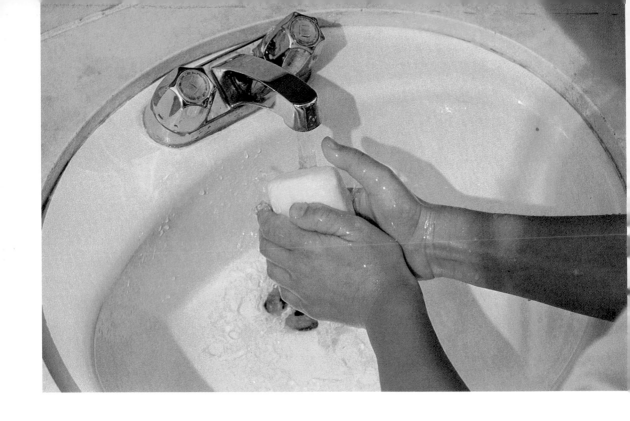

Remember to wash your
hands BEFORE you eat.
Use soap and warm water.
Also, brush your teeth
right AFTER you eat. The
more often you brush, the
better.

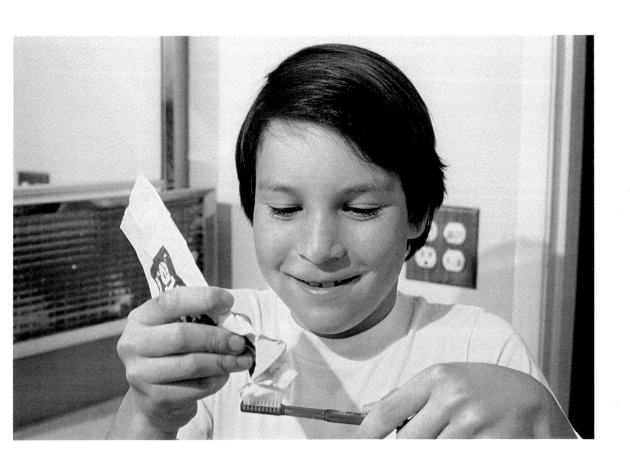

Taking good care of
yourself is a full–time job.
You have to do it all day,
every day.

When you are reading, take care of your eyes. Use a good light and sit up in your chair.

When you are walking up or down stairs, stay to the right. Hold onto the railing and watch your step.

When crossing the
street, wait for the signal.
Then look both ways, to
make sure it is safe.

When riding in a car,
use your seat harness. Try
not to bother the driver.

In a bus, sit in your seat
and be quiet. Do what the
driver tells you.

Wherever you are...

Whatever you are doing...

You are in charge of you.

Keep yourself safe and healthy, and have a good time.

WORDS YOU SHOULD KNOW

active (AK • tiv) —full of energy; busy; moving.

bend—lean over; to move part of the body lower.

brain (BRAYN) —human mind; the part of the body in the skull which controls the body.

breakfast (BREK • fest) —first meal of the day.

charge (CHARJ) —control; care.

clothes (KLOHS) —body coverings; garments.

contain (kun • TAYN) —to have in it; hold.

dessert (dih • ZERT) —last part of lunch or dinner.

energy (EN • er • jee) —power to do work; strength.

exercise (EKS • er • syz) —activity; to use the body.

grain (GRAYN) —the seed of corn, wheat, rice, and other cereal plants.

harness—strap to hold you.

healthy (HEL • thee) —in good health; not sick.

human (HYU • men) —person.

idea (eye • DEE • uh) —a thought.

important (im • POHR • tent) —have great value or meaning.

layer (LAY • er) —one on top of another; thickness.

lift—to raise.

loose—not tight; free.

muscle (MUS • il) —parts of the body that help in movement.

protect (proh • TEKT) —keep safe; guard.

railing (RAY • ling) —the support which you hold when walking on stairs; banister.

serving—portion; helping.

signal (SIG • nul)—warning.

special (SPESH • ul)—different from other kinds.

start—begin.

stretch (STRECH)—reach out.

strong—have energy or power.

supply (suh • PLY)—amount.

twice (TWYS)—two times.

wonderful (WON • der • ful)—very good; enjoyable; marvelous.

INDEX

About the Author

Karen Jacobsen is a graduate of the University of Connecticut and Syracuse University. She has been a teacher and is a writer. She likes to find out about interesting subjects and then write about them. She says, "Finding out about good health habits is especially interesting, because it means finding out how to take good care of oneself, . . . and that's important!"